David He No Fear

David He No Fear

By LORENZ GRAHAM

Pictures by ANN GRIFALCONI

Thomas Y. Crowell Company, New York

By the Author:

David He No Fear
Every Man Heart Lay Down
God Wash the World and Start Again
A Road down in the Sea

L.C. Card 71-109898

ISBN 0-690-23264-0

0-690-23265-9 (Lib. Ed.)

1 2 3 4 5 6 7 8 9 10

These little poems . . . are told here in the words and thought patterns of a modern African boy who does not . . . use the conventional words and phrases which by long usage often obscure the meaning of these tales in the minds of Europeans and Americans. This is the stuff of which literature is made. . . .

—W. E. B. Du Bois

From the Foreword of *How God Fix Jonah,* a collection of stories from the Bible retold by Lorenz Graham, in which David He No Fear first appeared.

Introduction

The familiar Bible stories of kings and slaves, of strength and weakness, of love and hate were brought to Africa by missionaries. As they were retold by Africans, they took on the imagery of the people. Shepherd David with his harp of many strings, strong man Samson who was weak for woman palaver, and baby Jesus born in the place where cattle sleep are now part of the folklore of the country. To the African storyteller the Bible tale becomes a poem, or rather a spoken song. His words are simple and rhythmic. The song is sung, and it is sweet.

It was in Liberia that I first heard many of these tales, recounted in the idiom of Africans newly come to English speech. They can be heard in many other parts of the continent as well—in the west and even in the east, wherever the English settlers spread their language.

Words of Spanish and Portuguese still remain on the African coast. *Palaver* now means something more than *palabra,* or "word." It can mean business or discussion of trouble. When "war palaver catch the country," people must fight, and some must die; and "woman palaver" often lands a man in jail. *Pican,* for baby or son or child, comes from *pequeño* ("small") and *niño* ("child"). The two words flowed together in English speech to become first *picaninny* and then *pican.*

Read again an old story. Behold a new vision with sharper images. Sway with the rhythm of the storyteller. Feel the beat of the drums.

> Long time past
> Before you papa live
> Before him papa live
> Before him pa's papa live——
>
> Long time past
> Before them big tree live
> Before them big tree's papa live——
> That time God live.

*To my father and mother
who also used to love to listen to
the African storytellers*

David *He No Fear*

David mind the sheep for him pa.
Every day he drive the sheep
He find good grass
He find sweet water
He mind the sheep good.

Bye-m-bye the war palaver catch Judah country
And all the mens must go.
The young men
The strong men
Take up spear and cutlass
And they go.

David's brothers go
But David self no be a man
So he stay by and mind the sheep,
David and him pa.

Bye-m-bye the word come back
The word say war go bad for Judah.
The word say other people be strong too much
And giant be for their side
No Judah man can fight him.
And David hear the word.

David go fore him pa face.
He say
    "Pa,
    Make it I go find my brothers.
    Make it I carry them chop
    They can be hongry this time."
The old man say "I agree."

When David come to the place
He walk about to find him brothers
And while he look he hear somebody say
    "Oh! One man make war for we!"

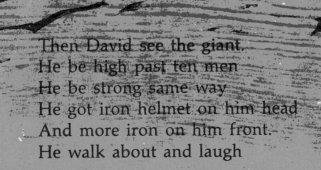

Then David see the giant.
He be high past ten men
He be strong same way
He got iron helmet on him head
And more iron on him front.
He walk about and laugh

He say
"Ho-ho-ho!
Them funny Judah mens!
They no can fight.
Come out now so I kill you
And if you no can fight
Go home and find you mommies.
Ho-ho-ho!"

And Judah mens do fear for true.
The Judah mens they fear to fight the giant
But David, he no fear.
David take him sling
He pick up round hard rocks
He walk out fore the giant and say
    "We God going fight for we!"

The giant say
    "Ho! Small boy done come to say how-do."
David say
    "I come for fight!"
Giant say
    "Do you mommy know you out?"
David say
    "Now I kill you!"
Giant say
    "Go from my face less I eat you!"

David stand.
He put rock in him sling
He turn it all about and round and round
The giant coming close
The sling leggo.
Hmmmmm. . . . . .Bop!

The giant holler out
He hold him head
He turn.
He try to walk
He fall.
He roll
He twist about
He die.

David walk up close
While all the Judah people shout
And all the other people run.
David take the giant cutlass self
And cut the giant head from off him neck.

Then David's brothers come and say
    "You fool!
The war palaver be for men.
Go home!
Go home and mind the sheep."

And David say "Now I go."

About the Author

Lorenz Graham was born in New Orleans, Louisiana, the son of a Methodist minister. He attended the University of California at Los Angeles for three years, then went to Africa to teach in a Liberian mission school.

Mr. Graham became interested in the tribal culture of his students and wanted to write about the African people. He returned to the United States and was graduated from Virginia Union University. Later he did postgraduate work at the New York School for Social Work and at New York University. He has worked with young people as a teacher and a social worker.

The author met his wife in Liberia, where she also was a teacher. They make their home in southern California and have traveled extensively in Africa and the Far East. Most of Mr. Graham's time is now given to writing.

About the Artist

Ann Grifalconi has always been interested in the special qualities of different cultures, qualities that can be seen reflected in the way a particular culture understands and tells the great stories of the Bible. What could better suit this interest than DAVID, HE NO FEAR?

In order to capture the special African flavor of this story and to picture what she thought the original African storyteller saw in his mind, Ann Grifalconi chose woodcut as her method of illustration. Woodcut is, she feels, the simplest, the strongest, and the most traditional of methods.

Miss Grifalconi is truly a New Yorker. She was born in New York City, and is a graduate of Cooper Union and New York University. She has taught in the city's junior and senior high schools, and she still makes her home there.